Pioneer Spirit
The
Westward
Expansion

THE
LOUISIANA
PURCHASE

Rachel Lynette

PowerKiDS
press™
New York

For Emily

Published in 2014 by The Rosen Publishing Group, Inc.
29 East 21st Street, New York, NY 10010

First Edition

Editor: Jennifer Way
Book Design: Greg Tucker

Photo Credits: Cover, p. 14 Courtesy of the Collection of the Louisiana Historical Society at the Louisiana State Museum; p. 5 Photos.com/Thinkstock; p. 7 Architect of the Capitol; p. 8 Sam Pierson/Photo Researchers/Getty Images; p. 9 Linda Steward/E+/Getty Images; p. 11 Hippolyte Delaroche/The Bridgeman Art Library/Getty Images; p. 12 U.S. National Archives and Records Administration; p. 13 Photo Researchers/ Getty Images; pp. 15, 19, 22 Kean Collection/Archive Photos/Getty Images; p. 16 MC_PP/Shutterstock.com; p. 18 Jason Patrick Ross/Shutterstock.com; p. 19 MPI/Archive Photos/Getty Images; p. 21 © SuperStock; p. 22 Transcendental Graphics/Archive Photos/Getty Images.

Library of Congress Cataloging-in-Publication Data

Lynette, Rachel.
 The Louisiana Purchase / by Rachel Lynette. — 1st ed.
    p. cm. — (Pioneer spirit: the Westward expansion)
 Includes index.
 ISBN 978-1-4777-0781-4 (library binding) — ISBN 978-1-4777-0895-8 (pbk.) —
ISBN 978-1-4777-0896-5 (6-pack)
 1. Louisiana Purchase—Juvenile literature. 2. United States—History—1801-1809—Juvenile literature.
 3. Napoleon I, Emperor of the French, 1769-1821—Relations with Americans—Juvenile literature. 4. United States—Territorial expansion—Juvenile literature. I. Title.
 E333.L97 2014
 976.3'01—dc23
                          2012044925

Manufactured in the United States of America

CPSIA Compliance Information: Batch #S13PK6: For Further Information contact Rosen Publishing, New York, New York at 1-800-237-9932

CONTENTS

The Louisiana Purchase

After the **American Revolution**, the United States reached only from the East Coast to the Mississippi River. Then, in 1803, President Thomas Jefferson bought a huge area of land in North America from France. This land was called the Louisiana **Territory**. Now the United States owned most of the land from the Mississippi River to the Rocky Mountains.

People soon began to settle on this new land and the United States grew quickly. By the turn of the twentieth century, the country had been settled from the Atlantic Ocean to the Pacific Ocean. This period of growth is called the **westward expansion**.

Thomas Jefferson authorized, or approved, the purchase of the Louisiana Territory from France. He was not the person who worked out the deal with that country, though.

A Growing Nation

In 1783, the United States won the American Revolution against Great Britain. At this time, the newly **independent** country was made up of 13 states and territory that stretched from the East Coast to the Mississippi River.

After the war, more people **immigrated** to the United States from Europe. Many of them settled between the Appalachian Mountains and the Mississippi River. By 1803, four more states had joined the country. Some Americans wanted to settle west of the Mississippi River. Most did not go because that land, called the Louisiana Territory, was owned by Spain.

Fighting in the American Revolution ended with the Battle of Yorktown. This painting shows the British general Lord Cornwallis (center) surrendering to the American general George Washington.

An Important City

At the beginning of the nineteenth century, the Louisiana Territory was owned by Spain. This territory was 828,000 square miles (2,144,520 sq km).

The Cabildo, shown here, was the seat of New Orleans' government when it was owned by Spain. It still stands today.

This nineteenth-century engraving shows New Orleans' busy port. Ships carried goods along the Mississippi River.

The Louisiana Territory included the city of New Orleans. New Orleans was an important port for American trade. Americans who lived west of the Appalachian Mountains could not easily move their goods over the mountains to be sold. Instead, they used the Mississippi River to move them. Spain allowed them to store their goods in warehouses in New Orleans until they could be shipped elsewhere. Even so, there were people who hoped that New Orleans could one day be part of the United States' territories.

France Takes Over

In 1801, Spain signed a **treaty** with France. This treaty gave the Louisiana Territory, including New Orleans, to France. After the treaty went into effect, Americans were no longer allowed to store their goods in warehouses in New Orleans.

The American settlers were upset about the changes in the port rules. They blamed France's leader, Napoleon Bonaparte. Thomas Jefferson, the president of the United States, did not want to fight with France over access to the New Orleans port. He sent a **diplomat** named Robert R. Livingston to Paris to try to buy New Orleans from France.

Napoleon Bonaparte

Napoleon Changes His Mind

When he first met with Robert R. Livingston, Napoleon refused to sell New Orleans to the United States. However, France was at war with Great Britain and needed money. Napoleon soon realized that selling the territory would give France the money it needed to keep fighting the war.

Jefferson sent James Monroe to Paris to help Livingston make a deal with Napoleon. Monroe and Livingston were surprised to learn that Napoleon wanted to sell the whole territory rather than just New Orleans.

This is the treaty for the Louisiana Purchase.

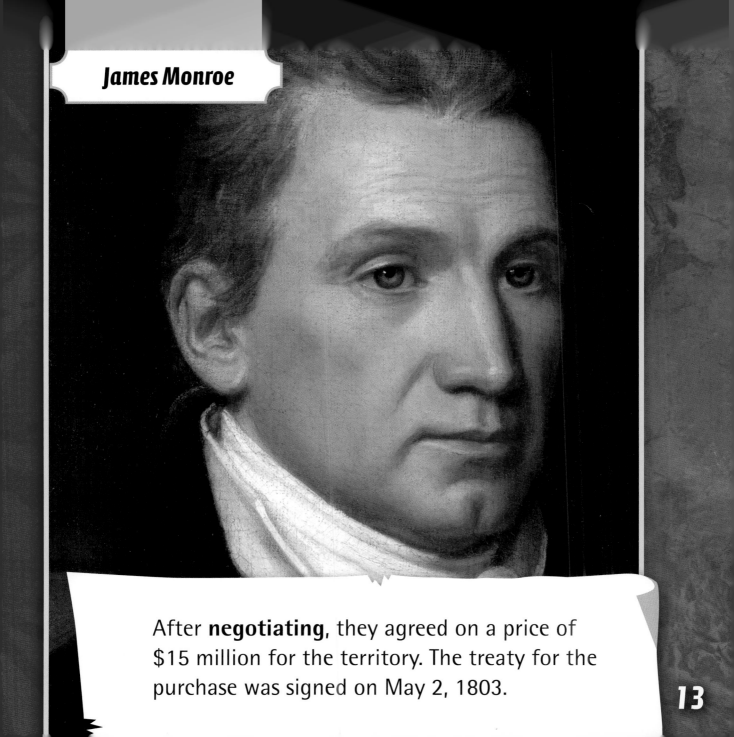

James Monroe

After **negotiating**, they agreed on a price of $15 million for the territory. The treaty for the purchase was signed on May 2, 1803.

Problems with the Deal

The news of the treaty reached the United States in June of 1803. President Jefferson was surprised to learn that the United States had bought the whole territory instead of just New Orleans.

This painting shows the ceremony in New Orleans during which the power over the Louisiana Territory changed from France to the United States. The French flag is being lowered and the American flag is being raised.

Congressman John Randolph of Virginia was one of several members of the House of Representatives who opposed the Louisiana Purchase.

Not everyone was happy about the purchase. One reason was that the United States would have to borrow money from other countries to buy the territory. Many people believed it was a bad idea to buy so much land without exploring it first. Other people questioned whether the **Constitution** gave the president the right to make the purchase. Despite these concerns, the United States Congress approved the treaty in October, 1803.

Valuable New Land

By purchasing the Louisiana Territory, the United States more than doubled its size. This made it one of the world's largest countries. Americans who had worried that the unexplored wilderness was mostly swampland were soon proved wrong. After it had been explored, much of the Louisiana Territory turned out to be good land for farming and rich in **natural resources**.

A lot of land gained in the Louisiana Purchase had rich soil suitable for farming. This farm grows corn on that soil in Iowa.

Map of the United States 1803

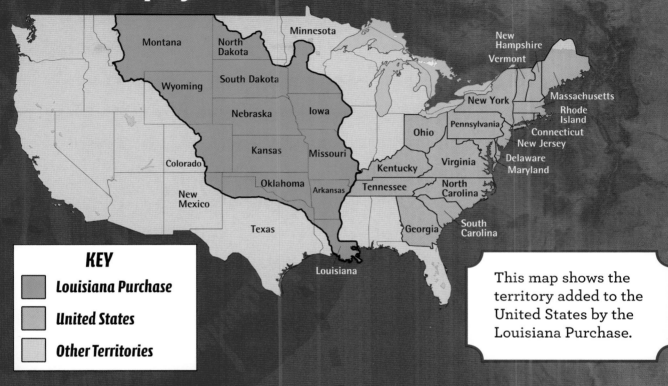

KEY
- Louisiana Purchase
- United States
- Other Territories

This map shows the territory added to the United States by the Louisiana Purchase.

This eventually helped make the United States not only a bigger country, but also a richer one. Over the next 90 years, the Louisiana Territory would become part of 15 new states. These states stretched from Iowa, Missouri, and Arkansas all the way to Montana and Wyoming.

Time to Explore

On May 14, 1804, Jefferson sent Meriwether Lewis and William Clark to lead an **expedition** of about 50 men into the Louisiana Territory. They were instructed to report on the land, plants, animals, natural resources, and people who lived there. They were sent so that the United States could learn about the territory that had just been bought.

Bighorn sheep are one of the many then-unfamiliar animals that Lewis and Clark described in their journals.

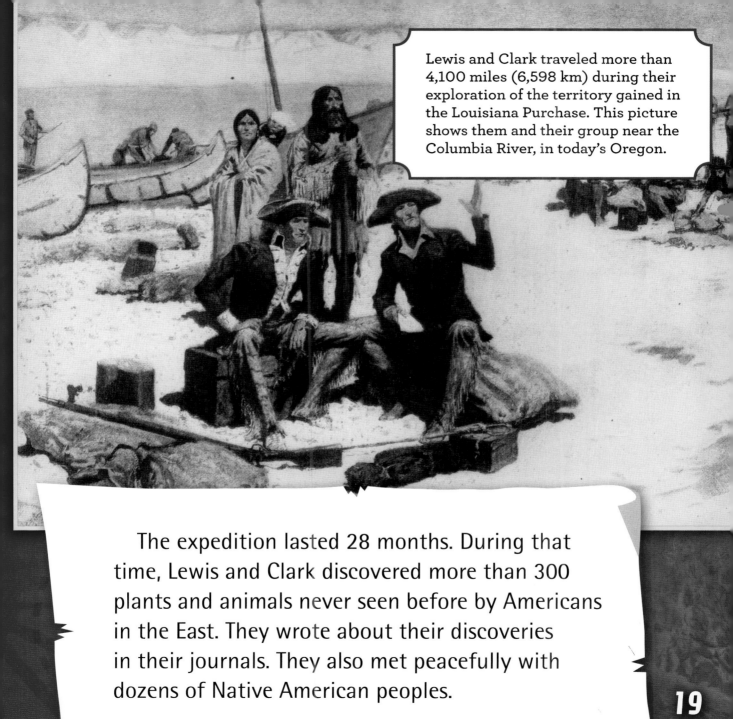

Lewis and Clark traveled more than 4,100 miles (6,598 km) during their exploration of the territory gained in the Louisiana Purchase. This picture shows them and their group near the Columbia River, in today's Oregon.

The expedition lasted 28 months. During that time, Lewis and Clark discovered more than 300 plants and animals never seen before by Americans in the East. They wrote about their discoveries in their journals. They also met peacefully with dozens of Native American peoples.

Taking the Land

After the United States made the Louisiana Purchase, Americans began to settle on the new land. Native Americans were already living on much of this land, though.

The United States government took over the Native Americans' land in American states and territories, often by force, and made them resettle elsewhere. Many were killed or died from diseases brought by the settlers. In 1838, 15,000 Cherokees were forced to leave their land and walk 800 miles (1,287 km) to be resettled. One-quarter died on what is now called the Trail of Tears. The United States' treatment of Native Americans was one of the bad effects of the period of westward expansion.

This painting shows the forced relocation of the Cherokee Native Americans on the Trail of Tears.

To the Pacific!

Many people moved to the Louisiana Territory in the 1800s. In the south, many of these people were slaves. Although these slaves had no rights, they did much of the work of settling this new land.

The Louisiana Purchase marked the beginning of the westward expansion period in American history. At that time, many Americans believed that America should someday stretch from the Atlantic to the Pacific Ocean. Purchasing the Louisiana Territory was the first step toward making that dream come true.

The Louisiana Purchase began the period of westward expansion in the United States. This period lasted through the rest of the nineteenth century.

GLOSSARY

American Revolution (uh-MER-uh-ken reh-vuh-LOO-shun) Battles that soldiers from the colonies fought against Britain for freedom, from 1775 to 1783.

Constitution (kon-stih-TOO-shun) The basic rules by which the United States is governed.

diplomat (DIH-pluh-mat) A person whose job is to handle relations between his or her country and other countries.

expedition (ek-spuh-DIH-shun) A trip for a special purpose.

immigrated (IH-muh-gray-ted) Moved to another country to live.

independent (in-dih-PEN-dent) Free from the control of others.

natural resources (NA-chuh-rul REE-sors-ez) Things in nature that can be used by people.

negotiating (nih-GOH-shee-ay-ting) Talking over terms for an agreement.

territory (TER-uh-tor-ee) Land that is controlled by a person, group of people, or government.

treaty (TREE-tee) An official agreement, signed and agreed upon by each party.

westward expansion (WES-twurd ik-SPANT-shun) The continued growth of the United States by adding land to the west and having settlers move onto it.

INDEX

WEBSITES

Due to the changing nature of Internet links, PowerKids Press has developed an online list of websites related to the subject of this book. This site is updated regularly. Please use this link to access the list: www.powerkidslinks.com/pswe/louis/